Dangers

THE HOUGHTON MIFFLIN
NEW POETRY SERIES

Judith Leet, *Pleasure Seeker's Guide*
David St. John, *Hush*
Heather McHugh, *Dangers*

Dangers

POEMS BY

Heather McHugh

HOUGHTON MIFFLIN COMPANY BOSTON 1977

Library of Congress Cataloging in Publication Data
McHugh, Heather, date   Dangers.
(The Houghton Mifflin new poetry series)   I. Title.
PS3563.A311614D3   811'.5'4   76-30645
ISBN 0-395-25180-X   ISBN 0-395-25175-3 pbk.
Printed in the United States of America

W 10 9 8 7 6 5 4 3 2 1

Magazines and anthologies in which the following poems previously appeared are: *Harper's Magazine:* "Refusal to Be Two-Timed," "Excerpt from an Argument with Enthusiasts Concerning Inspiration," "Spinster Discourses on the Natural Sciences." *The New Yorker:* "Divorce," "Corps d'Esprit," "It is 70° in Late November. Opening a Window You Nearly Know," "Spectacles." *New American Review:* "Housewife" (under the title "House-wifery"), "Recip-," "Night Catch" (under the title "At Night"). *American Poetry Review:* "Against a Dark Field," "At the Oysterbeds, at Low Tide, the Groom Addresses His Bride." *Seneca Review:* "Pupil," "Note Delivered by Female Impersonator," "A Nova Genesis." *Antioch Review:* "Ozone," "Peacemaker," "Lessons for Slow Learners, Poets, and Moons," "Leaving," "Knowing the Score" (under the title "Playing the Numbers"), "Making." *Antaeus:* "Double Agent." *The Atlantic Monthly:* "Having Read Books." *The Nation:* "Fido," "Sleep, after the Ray Charles Show and Hurricane Report." *Twelve Poems:* "Artist Shooting Quail, Early Fall." *Pequod:* "What the Palmist Knows," "Address." *Southern Poetry Review:* "Tendencies." *Ardis Anthology of Contemporary Poetry:* "YWCA." *The American Poetry Anthology* (Avon Books) reprinted "Corps d'Esprit," "Night Catch," "Note Delivered by Female Impersonator." *Loving, Living, Dying* (Scholastic Press) reprinted "It is 70° in Late November. Opening a Window You Nearly Know." *White Trash* (New South Co.) reprinted "Leaving."

For my lovers
For Grischa

Our interest's on the dangerous edge of things . . .
BROWNING, "Bishop Blougram's Apology"

ACKNOWLEDGMENTS

I made it, but I had help. Thank you,
MacDowell Colony, National Endowment
for the Arts, friends in the community of poets,
music- and shapemakers, all those people who
showed me the loving ropes.

CONTENTS

I. BLACK GLASS

II. PUBLIC PLACES

III. DOING TIME

I. Black Glass

Spectacles

I don't move
but the grass spreads in the window
its smear campaign. Trees revert
to wet green, and the irises

bearing the saliva of high shine
cast even the mud of what I can see
blue with a colorfast blood.
I am no longer a man of distinction:

my window fills with resemblances,
a face like mine, an evening's
long damp beard like lawn, the paperboy
who wheels familiarly across

my paired paned eyes, appearing
only to leave warped tracks. This is no
news, good news. I don't move
in the dark. My wire-rimmed glasses

sprawl on the desk, either a bright
suggestion to the uncorrected
eye, or a small
wrecked bicycle.

Night Catch

The wise fish digs his silver
in to the sludge at the late
fisherman's bait of lantern.
No light nudges him upward: tail and fin
refuse to flicker and the old old yearning

blackens in the place of burning.
Mud becomes him, who drops out
of luminary schools. And you my brightest
educator must forgive my learning to live
in dives. I have made up all the whitest

things about me, they are lies. Absence
has a grace you misconstrue, invention
its blue space to tide hearts over. Recognize
the artifice of hate, its deep
black glass, the surface that the face

refuses to shine through.

Orbit

The woman with one glass eye
will cast no stones, will name
no sinners in the sleight-
of-hand show, knows
the house is in her head.
The eye's not quite
opaque; the world
is breakable. She buys it
anyway, its milk glass, brand
of shaking bed, line
of sweets and scenes
that do dissolves.

Tonight the moon is two

quarters, into which she moves,
reflective. Seeming
has a zero at its heart, and sum
and difference have put
their arms about
the woman with one glass eye.
She's half asleep, half keeping
watch, her dreams a dim
swerve and a longing and a wide
lens into which
distortion lets
a man's face sink or swim.

Sleep, after Ray Charles
Show and Hurricane
Report

A storm named for a woman
was born as a mild
disturbance off Africa.
It broke into interiors

of pianos, blew the tubes
of trees and went on
record with weed for its whistle.
Now, bystanding, I

come down with a blessed
attack of the dance. I am white
trash, brother, one more basket
case. You boss the winds

like nobody's business, but nobody
can bear or see himself.
Life is the mother
with murder in her eye, and we

are junked and treasured,
every one regardless.

Fido

A dog is lost.
Its owner's voice
and whistle warp
the dark. I might as well

have been alone forever
on the listen
side of doors and windows.
I can see the woman

in the glass, her head
tilted to yell, her hair
a conference of light.
I see the black toad telephone

crouch by her in a knot
of quiet, curling
the unsevered cord.
She is waiting for her name

to be called, or out
of an anger of insulated
wires or hair tangle or tongue
hanging out, out of doubled over, out

of broken glass, to come.

Blind Date

Finger by finger the cold makes its
appropriations: friends
leave the room, my shoes
are old, the room won't settle
for me. So I pull the wool
of freakhood over my eyes and huddle
my one warm cup and call for any little
intimacy, song or match. Humming

his sometime way
home from another coast, some
lover with a carload of kindling, my lover
of painstaking ways, will come
as no surprise. Forever will mean something when he's laid
the heavy coins of kisses on my eyes.

Pupil

A little person, I lean in your eye.
A language already translated, I rise
when you call upon me. I ride
the sea of your person like troubled sheep.
I am doubled in your image: every one is
two-faced. This is living, in
arithmetic or sin. Declining, I
am single as the moon that sinks and climbs
the walls. We keep refining grammars, keep
our senses. Certain bodies make for certain
tides. A little lean, I eat in your eye.

It takes a seer to know one. Men circle the earth, they eat
from east to west. Nothing pronounces them
alone. Not even sleep
goes unconjugated. Only I, inclining
like the sun, reverberate. A lot

of you, I lap and graze on your rocks.
A little me, I learn in your person.
When you point your finger, my mouth doubletalks.

Song of the Specialist's Ex

Sleet in the night has left
a glaze of generalities: we all
are on an equal footing now, none
too secure. I light a joint:
the match makes its brief pure
peculiar blue, and then the grain
is lost in glue, the glaze
in glaze, the mind in its
own losses. Where did you clear out to,

taking the fall, "the better
to see, my dear"? Slow tugs of consequence
have hauled, across my weeks, a barge
of dimwits, wide of mark, soft-headed
as a while of snow and sneezes. Now I miss the hard
times, when you turned on me
specifics of your smile: those points
of view, your pupils, learning
(within limits) to enlarge.

What Is Blind

This weather I must fight to stay
awake in, maybe, all these borderless
light grays that say the sky
is underfoot, the earth is not
on edge and soft
is blind and soft is general.
I have in you a hope
of landscape crawling
with design, rife
with sight; a scene
with instance idiot: a pointillistic
night, a punctuated dark, where all the cooler
articles of faith are stars; or fine
print in the figured
grass where birds
research a morning
turn of phrase and worm
articulation from the dirt.

We're far from that.
The fire has made of all the lawn
an entropy, an ease, a sprawl
of blind likemindedness,
the scratch and quill of independence
long since spun away
as sparks, the smoke
become the same
as snow, below, above, to swallow

all specific gardens I have kissed
of you. You ask me what

is blind and I insist.
Not love not
love not love.

Preferences

Antarctica is no place for the eye
that loves a mesh of interlacing, knot
of growth. The plain truth oversimplifies
the human state. The southern senses set
a trap of fictions: stick and wire to stir
up single-minded nature, complicate
the unanimities of cool with fur
and fine desire. The draftsman tolerates
no unassuming page, but goes about
unearthing all its bones; the ink insists
on fibulas and femurs, none without
the knob of trouble's ends, the double kiss
that terminates the clean sweep of the shaft.
The belly of a hill has got a fault
of birth corkscrewing inside out; the craft
of architects can make a skull or vault
out of a fever of ideas, the tile
details, and listeners warm to the song
when wildnesses are made to cool, to scale.
The heart's two-timing, thicketed and wrong
but reason doesn't simply make us single.
In the woodland latitudes we grow
to love the shrub's uplifted etch and tangle
over the amnesias of snow.

Knowing the Score

One puts on one's white socks,
one by one, expecting the geraniums
to stay put in the storm,
stay red in black weather,
saying nothing. One puts on
one's tennis shoes, though the only racket
is the Mediterranean's. One hears
the far uninterrupted alarms
of children as one ties one's shoes,
puts one's feet together,
opens the door and passes the plants
one favored once and potted, five
by five. One knows one's places,
seconds the sea's slant
on things, wants
the love one believes is native
to harm. Accountably

reaching the cliff one will unaccountably
dive. Upon reflection one will be two,
racing into each other's arms.

Ozone

These trees have the many circles of self-love.
Their leaves ring and ring and the fingers are fat
and the arms have a grab on the trunk, grove
in its own groove, moving as trees can get.

And what I cannot get around
(in which upside-down trees are hung)
is the cipher, the fact, of this pond.
It hugs and doubles what is upright and downgrowing,

as we may be said to be, and trees must.
Under rainfire my face in the water splits: above
and within transcription of my own cast
lines, I, I have the many circles

To See the Light

It is nothing till it takes
the window's rope of ivy, till it turns
the little envies face by face
transparent, till it infiltrates
and etches, makes the network float.
Vessels fill with light and rise
as weightless as suspicion: tissues
on a shrink's glass tabletop. Fixtures
of imagination. Filaments of my
current affairs. A man is waiting

close to catch my cry. He snaps a switch,
a tree of juice, a burning tree. I watch
what happens to the window's whip of living
shine: as stung as ever stunning, leaves
hang anyway on. It is their nature. I
begin to look at home. The whole room
trembles but I offer, lash
by lash, my naked eye.

In Praise of Pain

A brilliance takes up residence in flaws
that all the unchipped faces of design
refuse. The wine collects its starlets
at a lip's fault, sunlight where the nicked
glass angles, and affection where the eye
is least correctable, where arrows of
unquivered light are lodged, where someone
else's eyes have come to be concerned.

For beauty's sake, assault and drive and burn
the devil from the simply perfect sun.
Demand a birthmark on the skin of love,
a tremble in the touch, in come a cry,
and let the silverware of nights be flecked,
the moon pocked to distribute more or less
indwelling alloys of its dim and shine
by nip and tuck, by chance's dance of laws.

The brightness drawn and quartered on a sheet,
the moment cracked upon a bed, will last
as if you soldered them with moon and flux.
And break the bottle of the eye to see
what lights are spun of accident and glass.

Artist Shooting Quail,
Early Fall

Gravel pelts the belly of the car, getting
your metal up, making your gut feel
the common ground. Quail stay put
as you pass. You are always traveling

too fast for mechanical good and the birds
too slowly for their own. There are words
for days like this, a sentence of many
years. You will manage

yourself with no hands, face
yourself with no favor. Rounds
of ammunition will be sung by men
who want the music that can square them

with the world, until the only arts are those
of murder and of being killed.
The artist's wife is held
to his word, the trees keep color

up in arms, the bird
swallows the bullet, but none
will let the leaden
moment lead to gravity—periodic wife, trees

in heat, quail that will not start at cars
all light beside you, who won't stop at life.
In the rearview mirror, your imitator
hasn't the art they have, and does not redden.

His Lover Addresses Socrates

We have gotten modern but the moon still
arranges its floods. Rising and falling
on black, each field's made out,
distantly, of silver hair. Nightlong, fear

lashes at us from its moon-eye.

We lived once in a hemisphere where we
were not afraid of the dark, denied
ourselves each dose
of jealousy. But one

by one

in the mind's right
hemisphere ballooned
new white ideas: imagine we
are of two minds. Imagine I could make

you die.

We watch the night
serve up a mercury liqueur. Dog Star
goes dead quiet. Only far out,
on the rough dome of a hill,

can you hope
for the antidote: learn
to swim, burn or howl, when the water

levels your home, the hole
where the heart hangs out,

where the dog

turns on you, in you, his whine
a vicious wish, eye about
to roll. The moon
can dish it out. Don't hesitate:

drink straight from its bowl.

Floundering

Because I am lucky, I'm a glutton
for sea punishment this summer:
for the discipline of the current
    backlash, bondage

of the temporary. Underwater
every air is heavy, every somersault
a motion slowed. The sun's
    a warp, aware

as any sidewise eye with fins.
I sink past reckon's isle and past
the lace of debt and past the shell of
    work, wreck

of pleasures. Under pressure
I cannot tell green from blacking
out, or greed from sacrifice, from
    kisser killer,

sense from sense. The vessels lie
inside and out, belying
interface. The eye directly
    feels, filled

with how it looks. I dive
to prove this place, to know
how deep in my luck is the loving
    hook.

Letter

By the time the low light comes I'll be
in dark high places, making
my own envelopes and spitting
in the quill. The rules are: watch
where the leak of tobacco juice leads
on the dead man's face.
Learn how rivers grow to stem
and bushes flower in distinction
and the hands oppose the branch
of tears. The single truth is simply
false; the truth is never more
than an example. By the time

the low light comes instruction's glass
will have the bends. I'll know
the stone's vocabulary, correspond
with my imagined friends.

Lecture on Thanatos:
For a Leukemic Student

Never in full stride, the cliché,
half-mooning an eye, eviling a blade,
nor black came my worst friend, my own
best enemy. I shall decline.
I shall go on inversing till
my pupils grow too pale.

He minces, where I could not say
or name; has the nerve to invade
the heart of the tooth, to touch the bone
I should shake speech from. Mine
becomes his versatile vocabulary. We rehearse
our meeting. I talk to myself. The students fail.

Tendencies

A body is seduced by damages.
Swamp of bad blood, pump of glue,
it wants to wear a dress of bandages
and lose the human teeth and hair it grew.
Led on a leash to the penthouse rail it feels
attracted to the forty-story fall.
It catches in the wish itself. Or then,
unhaltered in the flesh's patch of all
thumbs, it will choke on mushrooms, soak its bones
before it thinks to suck and be sucked dry.
The man goes daily nose-down in the dead-
man's-triangle, to fill the purses of
his lungs with dirt. The normal child
will hold her breath, her own; will hear the sky
approach, and lurch from what she learned, and head
for what she'd otherwise forget. Defiled,
the body stumbles back for more; unloved,
it looks for luck; it comes when it is called
obedient. A woman, near the thin
ice of a man's regard will start, appalled
and partial, leaning in.

Excommunicant

Midnight sucks the tongues
of fire up the flue. Beyond
my darkened house move tribes
of electrocuted animals, the dry and foreign
scorpion, the porcupine with eyes that hiss,
stirring hot steel in pools.
Farther off, sea
salt and phosphorus throw
tantrums of blackouts and sparks.
Committing itself to moonlight, a murder of crows.

Let the hatchetman
wear his shock of feathers.
Let six women kneel when he needs
to piss, take breath
when he breaks wind. The sky
is starstruck, night a black-blue
moth with silver pins. And I

want company. I want a man
to remind me of all
the social laws, the laws
I once rejected. Supply
and demand. Cause and effect.
No sooner do I say so than
I hear, outside my door,

the telephone repairman
(dressed in black as black
as my desires)

pause to wrap the ends
of the wire around his hands.

Heredity

My mother grows emaciated
in the Danish modern chair.

I have fattened past the dotted
limits of my assigned space, my cells,

my DNA, and forget I was ever afraid
to speak. My mother cannot finish

a sentence. I know how to unwind
her helices of tears. I know

which hairpin keeps her
from going haywire, know how far

I'd have to walk to put
unwooden arms around her, hug her

till the struts shook. When will I see
you again, she wonders, adjusting

her glasses. Don't mention
your father. Marry the man

of my dreams. Wear my bathrobe
with its yellow leashes. Let me

love you, need you,
know you, let me

go. The things we cannot say
slip buttered knives through the venetian blinds.

She cleans her glasses, says beneath
her breath the town is not the same. My tongue

goes over and over
its old home ground, in which, today, were fixed

these two new slick
white stones, my own

false teeth.

For My Fathers

Down sifts a lunar
sand from lamps.
The languages

of smoke are spoken
by your mouth. You dump
a pipe's gritful into the half-

dismantled globe, ashtray
bought cheap as my knowledge
of trees. Outside

the sky is
overturned, a bowl
bitten with stars. The chimney keeps

transmitting, uniliterally, its code:
o,
as in no or something.

I can read lips: names
of your body alight
on my fingertips, no two

alike; your hair
is the transcription
of a laugh like mine

and in your face age
complicates
its ideograph,

a stroke at a time.
For now
we are content

to reinstate ourselves, say
something: nothing
can wait.

Adenosene Triphosphate

The light sinks on one, rises
on the other
side of the cell wall,
converted. I, who once
brooded on nunhood and was
afraid, grow bored
with ordinary beauty,
marry and leave the rabbi's
son, and wear bare feet
on floors of broken glass.
In the one remaining evening
window blooms a pale
distorted face: my housemate's
television. Looking out
for myself, I am superimposed
on the world, on edge
of sunset, brilliant bloods and bruise.
But even as I watch, darkness
arrives with its bundles, its black
gold lumps, its struggle
to reconcile far and near, to seal
the torn horizon. Give me strength,
lost gods, for the looking
glass, the glass
that scars and heals.

Terms

Ten below, and my ancestors
grow tightlipped in the grave
but keep their grip, but stand
their ground, their rocks
half frozen off, their eyes
as chipped and false as pyrite.
Underneath the snow's two tons
of sun, they bear me
malice, brandishing old trees.

I turn my back. An unscarred
meadow opens up, a stranger's
generosity, a brightness
empty of regard, a sheet
of listen. Listen:
I can see as far
as blind diviners do: past
January, past the accident
of kindnesses, past plan.

I'm my family's last.

II. Public Places

Squeal

She rides the last few minutes
hard, pressing her heels
in the stirrups, keeping
what she can concealed, a stone
hidden in a fist. But she's grown
too big, the room too cramped,
the body too well lit
with wet. A man has got a hand
in her again, he wants to pick
her pocket, leave her flat.
The room begins to heave, the white
elastic walls of senses wow,
the words well up, the skin
begins to give and give until the sheet-
rock splits, the last uncommon
syllable is leaking from her lips:
her body breaks in two. Spectators
grin. The sex is speakable.
The secret's out.

Park

This is the country
fied, or civilized: kept
lawns and keep off
signs, all the sprawling
come-on of the flowers
fenced. Fat man
in a sweatshirt. Boat
in a birdbath. Path
to the gate where the street
knives burn. The Angels
rev their bikes and wait.

I think I can name any animal here,
where the blue and the bright white
air of our unshaken innocence
is buzzed by a biplane
hauling slogans: Buy this
time! Pay those dues! Preliterate,
my kids gallop by on their own
tin stars, as ignorant as anyone
of love. It's only human,
and was never mine to lose, this
nature I thought I was rid of.

Gig at Big Al's

There is a special privacy on stage.
Wearing little, then less, then
nudity's silver high-
heeled shoes, I dance to myself: the men

posed below at tables
with assessors' gazes and the paycheck's
sure prerogatives are dreams
I've realized, my chosen

people, made-up eyes, my fantasies.
I pull down dark around the room.
I turn on sex's juke two-step.
I set foot on the spotlight's

isolated space and grease
my hips and lick my legs. With a whip
lash of gin in the first row anyone
can beat around the bush, can buy

my brand of loneliness, all possible
circumlocutions of crotch. No one
can touch me, by law
I cannot touch myself. So none

of it is public, not until
in one side door
on his soft shoes
my lover comes to watch.

Penitentiary

He is not his own man here,
in a room designed too small, with one
wall missing and one man in mind. The mind's

its own accommodation, gray. In either ear
a tangle of airwaves, tin cans of country
music, hard rock, soft sell. In either eye

the secondhand blues. Circular
argument, a clock returns
to where it started, scene

of the crime, nonstop.
He has not lost but lent
his senses to the state

(the commonplace) of mind. The sentence
runs on, simple. Now it's six
again. The cells grow thick

with energy confined. The ticker
doesn't skip a beat. The future is no more
ahead than is the past behind.

Kennedy Center

She puts her glasses on whenever music burns
her eyes or turns the light to splinters. Breakable,
her fingers find the cool assurances of stone
and throat; she stiffens in her fur and velvet
burrow, listens harder, learns herself invulnerable
in a fine-boned style. Her decorated husband's
senseless to the threat: he knows his manners, whatnots,
not to rustle program pages, not
applaud (when the stirred few do, unmannerly
but moved) between the movements.
His is a display of hearing, who has heard
he may tomorrow be a bureau chief. But the time will come

despite them when the best-
dressed listeners are touched
on the breast by a guttersnipe, when the stranger
sensuality stands in a jockstrap by the bed, when the end
arrives. That danger is the art: beneath
the tamest skins of glass and ornament
moves one deep peasant love
of trouble. Brother, at the break-in
everyone must play a part,
and you and I, and he and she, become
embezzlers at a moment's notice,
musclemen at heart.

Country Inn

The dining room is empty.
We are far from the town
of your friends, far from the mates
and former mistresses, amends.
The maitre d', whose only prey
we are, brings pickles, beans
in vinegar, and switches
on the musical not even he,
left to his own devices, wants
to listen to. My face is in the cup
of my hands. You consider it.
Around us a promiscuity of settings,
vainness of display; the white
sheets stretch untouched as far
as I can see. The fish will be
untender when it comes, but I won't
have the heart to say so; you will find
yourself, despite yourself, in my
apartment, wondering how long
my old man works. For now we make
the most of our opposing
faces. Waiters come and go.
You settle on a suitable
entrée, the room grows
huge, the afternoon
appears, a glaring
error, waste of windows. "What I hate,"

you say, "is public places."
The wine glass fills with sun,
a slow, bright bomb.
The mob in me sits still.

Econo-Wash

The sheets are written with illicit
wrinkles, my shirt has the sweat
of your work on it, socks, long
underwear, I haul it all off in a bag
to beat it clean and bring it back
anonymous two hours on. I am at home
in any laundromat, wearing
the sure disguise of my true looks,
half-given to the local revolutions, half
to a half-read book. The same old
strangers make the same
inroads and exits and reluctant
claims on my attention: cold air
at a doorway's whim relieves
the room's held breath. The wall
is glass, is made for steam and sight
to dwell upon, till everything is inside
out, a glove of the best
policy, a next-to-godliness. In each
tornado's convex eye, in each fat
churning watergate of suds, intolerance.
They'll have no dirty laundry here.
Love, we are washed up.

YWCA

Ex-Christian and sexophile, what
am I doing here? Mateless,
quarterless, too suddenly
consigned to frugality's
room at the top, a room
that looks out on the cityscape
I've missed too many years: strict
unpopulated zone
of slopes and tile. Inside,

the dead-designer-style
of single-mindedness:
one chair, one desk, one dresser, one
one-body bed. No evidence of loving
pasts, mess of relations,
father and son. I break
the rules and break out
my rye bottle. Soon

the room turns gold.
The window's inch of air admits
a vespered mile, incantatory
traffic. So the two-man god
has gone off-duty. So the habit's
been abandoned. So what? Here

the sun is setting
its aloof example: going down it grows
by a power of red: I see it

singularly balanced on the blackest
edge of hours or a roof. Let me
learn it now, lord: one
can be enough.

Institution

Late afternoon, in my adulthood,
I am put to rest in a sunlight
someone else has scrubbed, arranged.
The workers move far-off now, and make
their sensible edges of hum,
as lovers and presidents and companies
soundly mind the world's
remote machines. The earth turns
warm and motherly: I burrow

in her quilting of design
and randomness, allowed
to trust to time, mistake myself
in insight's one-way window, wait
until I know my place and am
what sunlight takes to, pane
by pane and shade by leaf and square
by parallelogram. As if

the world were safe.

III. Doing Time

Having Read Books

It is dangerous to stand in early fall
under apple trees in a field.
They will shoot you in the backyard
with fruit. It is dangerous to jack
the old car up in its old barn, and the baled
hay rotting overhead in its stall
is more dangerous than books. You come
right through the door into my house
with that seedy look, those eyes
green-gardened with intelligence, and some
deep danger in the way that you are learned.
I have stood under the trees,
borrowed time in the barn
and breathed grease,
and I am not about to turn
careful today. I grab your arm.
I drag you outside, without thought.
I take the risk of you in the hay's rot.

Stroke

The literate are ill-prepared for this
unmediated life: the day that turns
more tricks than a twisted tongue and is
untiable, the month by no mere root
moon-ridden, and the yearly eloquences more
than summer's part of speech times four. We learn
the buried meaning in the grave, the alphabet
in tracks of predators, tense in the slow
seconds and quick centuries of sex.
Unletter the past: the future comes to terms.
One late fall day we stumble from our study
for a song, and find the easy symbols
of the living room revised: the shocked
senses flock to the window's reference
where now all backyard attitudes are deep
in memory: the landscapes we have known
too well—the picnic table and the hoe,
the tricycle, the stubborn shrub, our home-
grown syllables of shapely living—lie
sanded and camelled by foreign snow.

Note Delivered by Female Impersonator

Perversion interests me,
a three-legged dog in the driveway,
Coquilles Saint-Jacques
on plastic dishes,
anything up the ass.
All I ask is a little
retardation. Let me be more
imperative: walk your holy
three-dots-one-dash walk
but not so fast. Serve
and order, shove and retract,
dump and lap, drill
and withdraw, but
slowly. Slowly.
Let me be more specific:
you interest me.

Promising Call Girl, or,
The Whore's Engagement

I'm going to settle
for you. I'm going to call
it a life, this grub

stake, stew
of us, this couple stuff, forget
the rubber lips, hip socks.

It will become my calling, calling
one and one enough. I shall begin to breed
contempt; I'll bore you

for your seasoning: rocksalt
and smelling salt, salt lick.
I shall domesticate the earth, be worth

my weight, I give you my embodied word.
I call my skull a kettle
full of us. I call myself a knee and knuckle mine for you

to burglarize. My name, the mud
somebody stirred behind my eyes, is me
and it will settle.

At the Oysterbeds, at Low Tide, the Groom Addresses His Bride

There is a grain of hate
in us, and it comes cheap, and we
suck up to it, spit shine
around, hope it will harden
and grow. The same glaze
rises in the human eye. To fall

for someone merely means to mate
two such eyes, merely to see
under the lip of another shell another sign
of cents, cornea of greed. Pardon
this. Love makes me say it, love will pay
the petty price, will buy the bitter beads. For after all

our bargaining together, a higher form of life takes us apart
and sells, as if it were precious, the stone of the heart.

Housewife

I want to be whipped again. Whole day
on the floor, upon my knees, stripping
them clean, while men sleep
in a nearby room. Dying
to please, pleased
to die, I wait
for someone to wake
up. Grab a strap. Do me in.

Outside in fact
the day is soft and not
a killer. Children
and noises slip on it
without falling. Where
have I been.

After a week the scraps begin
to rot right in the sink.
Can't be hip doing dishes, baby, flipping
plates, stacking the rack. I might as well
have wanted to be born
black, as be free of these wishes. Now

a door slams open. They begin
to stumble out, awakening
to want, to shake the kitchen down,
break open cabinets. They grub
and rummage, and drop

the empty cups. I hear
a curse like a ketchup bottle hit
the tiles and I
start taking off, I do start taking off.
Already one of them
is playing with his belt
as if it were a sweet thought.
Already I have fought and felt
the long line of its coming true and my
own coming and, across
my back, my whole
life humming.

Cape

You open the mons of your hand
with a clam knife. Blood dumps out,
the damn shells clamp down.

Your house is a fist against the hills
and the hills are bushed. You sleep
uncovered as a beach, and over time the gulls

begin to lose their footing on your face. The sand
grits its teeth. The ocean wants nothing
but to beat you up and one A.M.

out of the black
and blue you know you can't
live anywhere else.

Making

I wave to the whole sky
but the sea more loudly waves.
The sky plays with its clouds.
A lizard, tail half eaten off,
flirts with my shadow. I say
"Sun! Be serious!" It doesn't
know the differences. Two, three
days like this one, without rain,
the crops will suffer. Yesterday
some young American with lire
in his eyes made me an offer
on this damn land. I laughed
in his face. I said to my wife
"Make me a son." She makes me
a smile, the lizards in her face
all interweave. A son will double
her, then me. The earth jokes
back at us once in a while. The sun
is good trouble, like a lover.
We shall not leave.

Patronage

The gate posts where the drive
begins are foursquare stands
of stones that no one cut.
The mason found their fit and native
juttings, bite of related teeth, yin
and yang of rock, and set them there
to set, some hundred years, some limits
for an unencumbered life. I walk

my heavy shoes toward shelter, and the house
secures the very sense it flatters,
batting its shaded eyes, sprawling in parlances.
I will eat my words, be what I eat,
say what I see: the open door
unrolls its red tongue at my feet.

Politics

The dog pauses before the fire,
watches, gains
weight, can't make
light of it, lies
heavy down. Geese
freeze to the lake. The snake
wears a bad new wrinkle:
bark. The trees lie,
rustling skins, and squirrels
fib, the purses of their faces full.
The fire spits up its splinter
groups of dimes, of flint,
the arsonist is lying
here and there, the bear
begins to snore and every
outdoor animal expires
the rich white lie of air.
Even you are taken in.
It is not winter.

Peacemaker

This sea has been too goddamn
docile too long. Paestum hardly shrugs
in its dumps; the sun does
the same thing for centuries.
I would like to come from this bed
shared just too long, raving
and burning and spreading
the word: that nothing

is worth the saving but what
has wings and scrawls
higher than me. That the rest
must settle for a slow engraving.
That the purest peace would be
a black thick skin on things.

Recip-

The wind will rise and fall any number, any trick
of times by the time this is done. Bread
is a slow sure thing. The wind is in-
decisive: how high shall the season's
hems be, how much of an out-and-out
tousle the hair of hills and how degraded or adult-
erated or disturbed a given river?
Bread knows from the first
it will be double. Double.
There is my face

in its untroubled dough.
I know too much. I mind, I grow
to hate my looks which have
no sudden love-
ly changeability but sure
old age, and lunch is coming, custom-
ers and husbands to blow
the front door down. I know I must
move fast:

I take that gentle, willing
flesh and punch it, hard, with my fist
wherever I see myself. Then leave it,
just like that, fallen on a yell-

ow shelf. But through the afternoon
of scrap and talk I hear it
breathe, I hear it swell. I'll have

to face myself again, what is
never quite done, never outdone,
never done in.

Fable

The women are the makers of the men,
by hook and crook, by shuttle and by wool
of lifelong gathering. A dream supplies
a month of bundled sheep; a kitchen's fat
with fibs; the goat's to get. Long after dark
the men are raveled at a reddened stone
that beats back what cannot be seen, in kin-
dled twos, duplicity, the tongues of love,
the glossolalia of fire. The shoes
the men left empty after five will fill
with oranges of warm and talk of loose.
The women work their weaving into sleep,
the men are knit into the drowsy lie
that do is done and overly is deep.

And not until the tree of sons is lit,
and soup is turning brown upon the spoon;
and not until the yellow yarns are blue
and oil is risen reservoir to lip,
when art is burned on all their surfaces
will women find their calling in a moan.
And not until the noun has known the verb
(in grammars learned by heart and not by rules)
to slip particulars and fit, will gown
be nakedness and silver overall. And not
until they've spun nine spools of moon
will women lay their looming bodies down.

Fix

I.

I needle April into letting go: out of a white
all winter we mistook for poverty, the world
turns suddenly indulgent, dealing
pin and color wheels, springing
songbirds down buttered wires
and women wearing red wax lips
and dogs off-shrugging indoor months
like some uncomfortable fur. The senses
split their pods. The switchblades
hatch in the hands
of the nouveaux riches. The eye
gets flashy with superficial
wit, and jets flock to a big
blue bedroom, trailing their ribbons
of emission. Green

has made its inroads
in your eyes: you envy me
your skin-deep plain, the span
of your attentions. But when I unzip
your brown jumpsuit, your mise-en-scène,
whole baskets of pink and white carnations
tumble forth. My hands are full

of health, they tremble on the verge
of your having, the one

hooked eye to go, the undone
rainbow, prism of liquids, lip
of spill—

II.

Far and away
the strictest sun
is stationed overhead, lashes
instructed to keep an eye
on us. We don't look up
from loving. Therefore he,
hell-bent on pleasure, readies
himself to come: straps
on the fashionable
parachute and hums
a human tune. We hear him
hover in the season's wings,
the near obscene
old god, revving
his devil-may-care machine—

Domestic Song

In the space of my life I design such rooms:
I trim the air to music's measurements; I start
a fire in the fire's place; you are secure
in the double-chambered neighborhood
of loving, and the whole house raises
its cain of distinct
possibilities. Let us
have our differences: let go

wildness from its hold, the buzz and heat
of pleasure from its separate cells. The sweetness
is of paradox, intact, untouched, in the couch
of an accommodating hearth, in the nightlong
red-hot beehive we have started.

For Tad Miyashita, Who Makes Collages Out of Trashed Letters, Teabags, Firecracker Wrappers

Even a teabag's greater than its purpose,
soaking and slightly swollen, the old heart
steeping in the same old juice.

Falling in love is garbage.
You offer to make
tea, not believe. Not time. Not use.

After the fireworks, waterworks and brewing
have left us whole and heavy
evidences, short of art, you render them

lovely in their own undoing
                              weightless in the part

A Nova Genesis

Our history is touched
with gravity. The original penance,
it is the worst labor a lord
could impose. It is the name
of our lost agency. Everything we know
streaks downward, and we spend
the time of our life
buying heavy shoes, bankrupt
in leap years. Loaded
is our history with love. I want

to kiss you on the moon, be
borrowed light, and stage
new histories: no tides
in the ear and no such thing
as off-balance. I want to call
you by a name that will not stay on the page.
Raise parts of you up that will not fall.

Excerpt from an Argument with Enthusiasts Concerning Inspiration

I agree that something greatens us
but intelligence does not enter into it.
I can calmly say that when we turn certain
switches certain lights go on.
That there are rational tricks to make
things go away and things arrive.
But with whatever brilliance in the middle of the night

in whatever living room we sit down and discuss
what dead men know, things we can only intuit
breathe in the room. The curtain
fattens and collapses, fattens again. No one
hears his own voice. Yes, the mind is flashy, but take
the stupid wind away and say what's left alive.

Breathless is dead, however bright.

Reservation

Let me never weigh the handiwork
between us. Loving, gemini,
has for its lick and lash a fork
of tongues, for apple and for ache an eye.

I never want to know of your
endearment the dimension, so that on the cross-
hatched night our care turns up its paler
face, we cannot calculate the loss.

Because the voice has moored its pair of boats
in every skull's marina, and because the teeth
will raise no single issue on the lip, because our kids will float
us upside down, in time, in their two-timing eyes, because

on every hand the body packs
its double-barreled heat, don't number
passions. Do not ask
the caliber of loving, lest it name

a bullet after you. The measure
of your influence is feeling, countlessly again,
the senses fill the holes where pleasure
goes to father pain.

Lessons for Slow Learners, Poets,
and Moons

It is not what, but how. Flaying
must be done neatly, the strips
ripped straight or cut without
much fat caught underneath, whether
the landscape to be skinned is wrinkled
or young. As for love: with whatever

instrument, your tongue, held at
the cleanest inclination, drive
together argument and matter till you know
not what the matter is but how it shouts.
Divide the lips, wherever lips are met.
Take what you want, till women
climb the walls: knock them, using
metrics you have learned for tides. Remember:
lovely, ugly, once you are inside
they bleed the same. Command, if you would have
men rave or women howl, not words but ways

to make words heave in rhyme. Not who,
but how you touch. And they will slave

on your white hills. Pick up your pitch. Take your time.

What the Palmist Knows

The newspaper will keep, huddled
in its box. Snow dispenses
a soft aquatic dark to homes, the tame
cars creep into garages. Nothing

makes noise. Your five dogs named for senses
play alive, pillowing the air
with their paws. The snow drives off
the murderer but you

will pummel someone soon from speech.
At the door the latest
victim knocks with gloves. You know
the news already. Opening for her

your hands have their own
interrupted headlines.

Maid

Snow reclaims the woods with a vengeance, wanting
to make a clean breast of it, overlay
all carnal traces, matters of murder, evidence
of love. It's out to chasten bodies and deny
the mauled crow and the trap-foot fox, efface
all ideographs in black and red
of blasted texture and designing
bone. Beneath such absolutions
my dead dog grows clean
as a whistle with no meaning, till his truck-
struck pose in this white lie has lost
its guts and gist, its muscle. Don't give me

such morticians at the end, a con-job
that can camouflage alarm, refute the deep
red staining with a sheet or doctor
up the eye. Don't give me mercy for a friend,
a husband with a master bed to make
for good. I'd rather than fastened be fat,
unlocked than wed, undone than corseted
in white. I'd rather honor
in the flesh than hide
disaster's sprawl of substance,
bleeding's double bed.

Against a Dark Field

Hate makes my head light.
Hate rides its particulars, styled
after fireflies, after envy. My bed rises
on its liquid, I hate your

heavy-handed body right
by mine. The window's colony of wild
ideas, appointed, hovers. Wise
is lightweight. Undercover

I withdraw from you and turn
into pure fuel. You blacken with sleep. I green with burn.

Futures

It is an art
to market ungrown grain, create
in a mind's myopic
eye one gold,
and weight your pockets
with another. It is an art

to talk as if
poor possibilities
were presences, or promise
currency, as if the weathers without shine
could never jeopardize a seed
of the human power
to devise.

It is with artifice and fine
discrimination that the future-
monger moves from postulate to latency: given
someone else's trust, that rich soil
of presumption, he can plant
persuasively straight lines.
Take a poem, for example. It will trade
in hunger for a restless
literate disease, stake out

the fence around
what wasn't and what isn't, sink
your savings into fictions like tomorrow,

name the crops barely implied
in bare fields on the fence's farther side.
If you buy this, you're buying
time, by any other name
as borrowed.

Doing Time

I have put on
my pinkest cheeks, made up
this bed and inspired
naturally flat sheets with fit
speech. When you come, a simple
fiction on your hands and some
accustom worn as plainly
as pajamas, I can hear
my singularly dumb heart start
pretending to a number exercise.
When you climb in
tautologies get out:
our bodies, absolutely relative,
will settle for snatches
and pricks of giving. Having

my comforter, I glow; having your words
you ignite the oil lamp and begin to read.
Behind the face of the fake
clock our whole living
ticks and twitches. Love

is hate. Hard
is easy. What unholy
wisdoms we are getting we are getting
far too late. I watch the watch
on your wrist as it grows
its own lid. I see

the sheets deflate, the print
link lie to lie, the mirror
overhead disclose

light sinking in my hue,
light sinking in your eye.

Rent

The paint, peeled back, reveals
an oak past salvaging. Windows
are inside riddles, doors are out
of sync with jambs, the honeysuckled
stoop is true to nothing
but its name. This house

bends to it all it holds: and we
who live in bodies are about

to see what faces in the finish
we ourselves have leased: my own pent
up in pining, yours
unable to reside
in anybody's eye without diminishment.

Reprise

First we planned the family.
Then, one by one, relinquished
the song and dance of habits, hit
singles, swinging, wickedness
of things we did not need, quick-
silver and sand, time
off. You no longer
whistled in the morning.
I no longer fancied flight.

We bought bronze shoes.
We lost our tans. And in the baby room
we work our pinking shears
and blues. Today I sit
by the window and rock and knit
a net of futures. As I watch, a bird
in the ash, in the middle
of a morning's
gather-weave-and-stamp
work, nestwork, steps

aside, raises
a quiver of wishes
from a well-oiled throat and breaks
into twelve gold tones of ornament.
I am utterly stilled.
Fledglings fill
the mothering air, so many
feathers of invention,

so many shadows of coming, memories
of the South, they fall,
they measurelessly fall. She sings
for life, as if there were nothing
else to be done, as if there were no knowledge
in design, as if
necessity and pleasure could be one.
I sit, open-mouthed, on the edge of my chair.

Leaving

Between your lips trees grew like words.
Your tongue got too flowery. You went on
and on like Virginia, until I was unheard
of, a name plowed in your mouth for fertility to set upon.

I hope I never see anything grow
undisciplined, unshaped again,
dressing the cypress up in moss, in mud below.
I am not of your kind, the gentle men

who hold the wooden handles and the bare
blades of verbs, but do not mean them.
I am the new woodsman, who will spare
lives, thin them, lean them,

whack past gardenfuls of harvesters and hurt and have
in my heart an ax, in my mouth a word: desert.

Divorce

The cat walks on my body in the dark
as if it cared. I can't get out of my mind
that the stars have left tracks on
the floor. I see mates everywhere.

Lately, given to long walks and a certain park
I've gotten the trees to answer, in a kind
of finding. When I was little the lawn
could chatter through its blades, but there

and then we were allowed the voices we might need.
I should no longer believe in the angels I know
came down. But they are offspring,
to be seen and heard. I make my choice: I shall survive

my legitimate spouse for the love of the weeds,
for the sake of a cat, constellations, the low
wild expressions of trees. Before sleep, each night,

I am glad to see the ghosts arrive, bringing
no prerequisites for being alive,
and out of the dark a personal talking light.

Refusal to Be Lonely

It must be enough to make
friends with my body, to keep it
amiable as a cellmate, strong
as a subordinate, as true as human-
kind can be. I walk it till it shivers
in the wind. I work it till petitions
shake its hand. We read the redder
leaves together till we are
of one unflowered mind. At night it grows

on me, it chuckles at the grave, it loves
its overlord and dances
to my tyranny of tunes. It must

be underling enough: I'll have
no stranger slave.

Address

Naturally superfluous, the world breaks
out its green glut every spring. In the street
rain doubles the lights of chance
cars, and my frontyard grubs increase
in numbers and in appetite.
The world naturally overdoes
all hunger.

This month I have beaten that
fraction of a year (the dance
of thirty days of feet, the lease
of color) from the rug. I've chipped the bright
designing from the furniture of mind,
thickened and simplified the heart's assaulted wall.
Men, I live in a new house. Finding it, you find
a single-minded me, the me

no one will ever move again.

Double Agent

I pledge allegiance to the old
country, the hourless
state, the powers
of sleep. I was born to sleep,

its populations, floodgates,
déjà vu, its tunnels. I crave the escape
artistry of slaves, each neural
pathway with its shutter-quick
synapse. The mind is wicked, very well,

the judge is dead, the legislators
naked, and the plain girl has her hairlips
kissed by the rubber
sticks of pilgrims; her legs spread
rumors of deafmute victory; her fingers
and toes are written with scripts
no one can reproduce. No one keeps the time,

and watches stop, and monasteries
softly swallow men. My citizenship
is clear as unpolluted
airways, clear
as a carnivore's eye.
The girl gets the queen's

emissary wet, who comes bearing
bacon, a message
for me who read meat. The only remote

possibility, a bruise at the skyline,
fog at the edge of the world, is her
desire: the past she wants

is west, toward which a moon
or mood or metronome impels me. Only when
in some extremity the ship of the queen
or state is sunk or wrecked

on a radio wave do my own
eyes open to the dim
and human spectacles, my ears fill
with harsh insurrections
of kitchens, cash
of electric light, crash
of ungoverned dishes. The flag
I am wrapped in whitens
into sheets. Surrender

is arranged. I am at home. I am in time.
Another fifteen minutes and I'll write
world history, omitting every night. I rise

to the occasion of the bathroom sink, and foam
at the mouth, naturalized.

Corps d'Esprit

Just when you're able to admit
you always wanted to whack
her one with your backhand
hard, then some outrageous stroke
of bad luck, backstroke, does
it for you. Just

when you know what to do
with your life, the mother
of it and the wife you fixed
it up with, then it jilts
you all and crawls
off on your belly. Forty-two

is the number of years that fits
like concrete shoes. Just when you regret
your careless walking on the stream
of consciousness, the shoes remember and they haul
you in. What of your dry amusement? What

of your nonchalance? Just when you know
people best and have learned at last by heart
the logic of loving them least, just now

fish-eyed and heavy-footed in its wonder,
still fat in the fists of its intelligence, the body
of your life goes under.

Refusal to Be Two-Timed

I defy the Romantics, a poet is no prophet,
only less likely to be afraid
to disturb the time being, grab its wrapped gifts.
Child in the forbidden closet, I open things:
if the gift is good, I want
the ribbons off it;
if it's not, I want to know so
now, before the audience is there to lift
the lid with me, making believe, making applause.

Explicit morning light is celebrating little flaws
in the wooden floor. It must be my birthday.
I am an old grain in people, I am the sun.
Packages of shine are always waiting with our name
deserving to be undone. Beneath the tame
surfaces I can see wild
life: say, the varnished oak, turn-
of-the-century, illuminated here; or just outside,
that equanimity of snow, mild
humper of traps and carcasses, gentle necrophiliac,
with its occasional ornament of wrenched fur,
spat blood. Intimating spring, the sunshine burns

white holes into my room. It cannot misconstrue
the evidence. There is no application of shellac
it cannot see through; now it licks your
envelope and reads what you wrote, in such pleasant
terms, about the woman you had just
made love to, shares your sharing gift with me. My dear,

there is nothing, past or future, left
implicit here. I have unfolded
its paper fist, I accept
the present.

Debtor's Prison Road

I.

They always let me go at night, minus
my timepiece, lighter,
personal effects. Always
the air is shaking the same
jars of safety
pins: cicadas. Song
is recidivism: always
I'm abandoning the road to stand
in someone's field,
unwatched,
unseconded. The stars

that are not mine
tick fitfully, they always have
appointments. Punctual, six-sharp,
they are David's, and have lodged
in his death tent, have stuck
in his mud sleep. Bad luck

leaves me a loan: no company, no katy-
did or promissory
note or night
can last.
The air loses its nerve,
the old saw its eyeteeth and I
my words, my alwaysing and my.

II.

In hush the repossessors reach
the edges of the field, they pass

for shadows, sheep
of ambush, animals

of permanence, they turn
a black beyond returning and they haunt

the sleepless. I don't count,
who cannot earn my keep.

It is 70° in late November.
Opening a window you nearly know

how certain
days filter themselves through screen, chain
saw, sundust, games of chance.
How certain as cliché
certain days are. You make
a bed. Sunlight runs in. The bed
reconciles everything. You know

how the far-off can surround
you, how things swim
here thousands of miles inland,
of their own accord, in the unknown
passage of your human ear.
You know now how the times
at times can lose their most acerbic
edge, and your planned child and your grand-
mother rise as a sound
and single sweetness in the aural
shell you carry from amphibian history.
It is history

whose sharks sharpen the future.
You nearly know it. It is softer
carnivores, these days; it is the small-time
fisherman you are on shore, on edge
of rising, sinking
treasure; it's the mooning
of the earth, the measure

of your catch, this life you have
to scale, this little
gross and no net
worth. Momentarily
you will know
what you never have.

Spinster Discourses on the Natural Sciences

Axed
at the right point
wood snaps into strips
along its grain.
Rocks too
crack
along pre-extant tracks.
Weakest at the spine, down lines
of symmetry, the shell,
the skull
tapped by a gentle hammer, tell
the halves of life
beginning and life loss.

We are most vulnerable where last
we were conjoined: I hold this fact

in my fist
like a fifty-dollar bill,
like the future,
like the first
indivisible
egg.

Sympathy on Water Street

The dead end of the Eastport street
I live on is a haunt of young
and undomesticated couples who want
all night to throw themselves
for a loop, gear themselves
for the cul-de-sac, pay lip
service to the lovers'
leap. Ardently
their autos elbow-bump
and fender-bend, horns
blurt out, interiors glare as if
to publicize the feeling
up, the going down. I watch
from my window above
in the dark and can be
for all my decent distance
no more knowing. It's enough

to know our place, where the lay
of the land is the law: to the falling
off of solid ground,
to the infirm sea, that gutter
of comings and goings, we
who love inside are just
as perilously close.

NOTES

NOTES

PAGE

6 "Sleep": for Ray Charles, for whom dope and darkness were no impediment to rhythm and blues.

9 "Pupil": The poem owes some of its imagery to the cross-cultural linguistic studies of Sinologist Erwin Reifler.

10 "Song of the Specialist's Ex": Experimental evidence correlates pupil dilation and sexual interest (see Eckhardt Hess, Robert F. Hamel).

31 "Adenosene Triphosphate": ATP stores photochemical energy in plant cells, a sort of interlocutor between light and life.

37 "Gig at Big Al's": An ordinance governing topless-bottomless dancing in San Francisco in 1971 prohibited performers from "touching themselves."

91 "Debtor's Prison Road": for poets in prison, especially friends in Moberly, Missouri.